In Touch With Nature
Life in the Soil

BLACKBIRCH®
PRESS

San Diego • Detroit • New York • San Francisco • Cleveland • New Haven, Conn. • Waterville, Maine • London • Munich

PHOTOGRAPHIC CREDITS
Ardea: John Daniels 28–29; **Art Explosion:** 27, 30cl; **Image Ideas Inc:** 18–19, 22–23, 30bl, 30tr, 30cr, 30br; **Photodisc:** 1, 6, 13, 29tl, 30tl; **NRCS:** 4–5, 5t, 9, 10–11, 14–15, 17; **USGS:** 7.

Step-by-step photography throughout: Martin Norris

Front cover: Martin Norris and Photodisc

Consultant: Mark Hostetler, Ph.D.,
  Assistant Professor, Extension Wildlife Specialist,
  Department of Wildlife Ecology & Conservation,
  IFAS, University of Florida

For The Brown Reference Group plc
Editorial and Design: John Farndon and Angela Koo
Picture Researcher: Helen Simm
Illustrations: Darren Awuah
Managing Editor: Bridget Giles
Art Director: Dave Goodman
Children's Publisher: Anne O'Daly
Production Director: Alastair Gourlay
Editorial Director: Lindsey Lowe

LIBRARY OF CONGRESS CATALOGING-IN-PUBLICATION DATA

Available from the Library of Congress.

ISBN: 1-4103-0124-9

Printed and bound in Singapore
10 9 8 7 6 5 4 3 2 1

Contents

What is soil?

Soil is the layer of loose, brownish material that covers the world's land surfaces wherever it is moist or warm enough. The only places there is not much soil are in polar regions and mountains, in deserts, and in the heart of cities.

It is easy to think of soil as just dirt, but it is much more than that. Without soil, we would have no plants, crops, or food. Nor would we have any of the other vegetable or tree products on which we rely. Soil is also one of the richest of all wildlife habitats. The insects, worms, and other creatures that live in soil are mostly tiny and hidden out of sight. Yet there are more of them than in all the other environments of the earth put together. In fact, soil is a dynamic, living system. A whole range of physical, chemical, and biological processes go on in the soil all the time.

CLOSE-UP *Farming soil*

Through the centuries, farming and forestry have changed the nature of soils all over the world. In many places, very little soil is now entirely natural. Artificial fertilizers and pest sprays alter the chemical balance of the soil, for example. Plowing and tilling change the soil's structure. Intensive production of crops gradually alters the soil's organic content. The character of the soil is often changed even by irrigation. Irrigation is the process of directing water onto the soil so plants can grow better.

Did you know?

There is fertile soil on less than a sixth of the world's land surface, so soil is a fragile and precious resource.

CLOSE-UP *Air in the soil*

Soil is far from solid. Sometimes, up to half its entire volume is the space between the solid grains and clumps. Some of this space is filled with water. The rest is filled with air. Soil air is much like air above ground, but it has less oxygen and more of the gas carbon dioxide. Soil air is also very humid. The microorganisms and plants that live in soil rely on this air for all their oxygen needs. This is why they have problems when the soil gets saturated with water. Like surface animals held under water, they drown.

Soil may look solid, but is full of spaces. Some spaces are filled with air, others with water.

Soil is a surprisingly varied material. It ranges in depth from just a few inches to hundreds of feet. It has many differences from place to place. All soil, however, shares the same range of basic materials.

About half the soil is solid. Some of this is tiny fragments or grains of rock that are created as the rock below the soil is broken up by the weather. The rest is organic matter, the decaying remains of dead plants and animals.

The rest of the soil is air and water. These fill in the gaps between the solid matter. Finally, there are vast numbers of living things. These include the roots of plants that emerge above ground and countless bacteria, insects, and worms.

The good earth
Soil is a natural substance, but it has been changed by centuries of farming. Plowing the soil like this makes crops grow better. But it gradually breaks up the soil's natural structure.

CLOSE-UP *Crumbling mountains*

Mountain peaks like those pictured look tough (1). But even the toughest rock is eventually broken down by the weather. Water that freezes in cracks, for example, can expand so forcefully that it shatters the rock. Rock that is shattered like this tumbles down to form a slope of fragments, or scree (2) at the foot of the slope. As living things gain a foothold on the scree, the rock fragments are slowly turned into soil in which plants can grow (3).

Crumbling rocks

Did you know?
The scientific name for the study of soil is pedology. A soil scientist is called a pedologist.

Soil usually takes a very long time to develop. Occasionally, soil can form within just a few years. Soil often forms quickly on the ash produced by a volcanic eruption, for example. Usually, though, soil takes tens of thousands, or even millions, of years to form.

Soil typically begins to develop as a layer of loose sand, silt, and clay builds up on the ground. Sometimes, this loose material is carried, or transported, into place. It might be washed by rivers, blown by the wind, or pushed by glaciers. More often, though, it is made from fragments of the rock beneath.

Whenever rocks are exposed to the weather, they slowly crumble as a result of wind, rain, and cold. This is called weathering. As the rocks crumble, they form a thin coating, or regolith, over the surface of the solid rock.

Either a regolith or a pile of transported material forms what is called the parent material. Parent material is the loose material from which a new soil develops. A soil only truly develops once water, air, living things, and decayed organic matter are added to this parent material.

First, the loose parent material becomes home to a few plants and animals. Soon more plants and animals move in. When they die, their remains gradually get mixed in with the parent material. These organic remains will, in turn, form the food for a variety of tiny soil organisms.

CLOSE-UP *Soils from volcanoes*

It might seem strange that people choose to live near dangerous volcanoes. Yet the soils formed on ash thrown out by volcanoes are among the most fertile in the world. The minerals in them are very nutritious for plants, so crops grow well. What is more, the soils form quickly. This is because the parent material, the volcanic ash, is fine and crumbly, so it is easy for plant roots to gain a foothold in it. Volcanic soils can be fully formed in just a few thousand years. Other soils take much, much longer to form. Soils that form on volcanic ash are called andisols. There are andisols in Washington and Oregon, and also in southern Italy, Japan, and Indonesia.

Life like this fungus quickly gets a foothold in the ground after a volcanic eruption.

What's in soil?

Soils are complex materials made from four elements. First, there are solid fragments and broken down living matter. Then there is air and water in the spaces in between. Solid fragments are either broken bits of rock, or minerals, which are grains of natural chemicals. Broken down living matter is dark brown or black in color and called humus. All soils have these basic ingredients, but vary in color and texture. Differences in color depend on the amount of iron and other minerals in the soil, plus the amount of humus. Variations in texture depend on the size of the rock fragments. Soil scientists describe the tiniest fragments as clay or silt, the next biggest as sand, and the biggest as gravel. This project shows how to find out what is in your backyard soil.

TESTING SOIL ACIDITY

You will need:

✔ **A soil sample**
✔ **A wide-mesh gardening sieve**
✔ **A fine-mesh sieve**
✔ **A trowel for digging out samples**
✔ **A magnifying glass**
✔ **Bowls and trays for catching soil**
✔ **Tweezers**

Did you know?
Expert gardeners can tell the texture of a soil by rubbing it between their fingers.

1 Spread your sample of soil out on a tray. Then examine it closely with a magnifying glass. Take out plants, live insects and other animals, and animal bodies. Put them in a bowl.

2 Tip all the soil into a gardening sieve with a wide mesh. Shake it all through onto a tray. Pour the coarse material left in the sieve into another bowl, or tray.

Gardeners need to know their soil. Here, a soil expert is comparing different soils.

3 Pour all the soil that came through the wide-mesh sieve into a fine-mesh sieve. Shake it all through. Pour the medium material left in the sieve into another bowl, or tray.

Four grades
Sieving the soil in stages like this shows that every soil contains three grades of material, as well as living and dead matter. There is some fine material (silt and clay), some medium (sand), and some coarse (gravel). The proportion of each varies from soil to soil.

The amount of air and water the soil holds depends on its texture. A coarse textured, gravelly soil contains much more air than a fine textured soil. Clay and silt soils, on the other hand, tend to get waterlogged. This is because, in clay and silt soils, the grains are so tightly packed that water cannot drain easily. The wetness also makes grains stick together in huge lumps, or clods. The wetness and stickiness of clay and silt soils makes them hard for gardeners to cultivate: that is, dig in and grow things in. Sandy and gravelly soils are much easier to cultivate, but tend to dry out quickly. The best soils are loams. Loams contain both sand and silt.

living and dead matter

medium material (sand)

fine material (silt)

coarse material (gravel)

9

Different kinds of soil

Soil is usually brownish and made of the same basic ingredients, but it varies from place to place. Different soils form on different kinds of rock, for example. Soils can vary with the landscape, too. On steep slopes, soil and its nutrients are easily washed away by rainwater, so soils tend to be thin and infertile there.

The nature of a soil depends mainly on the climate and the plants growing in it. Where it rains heavily, grains of natural chemicals, or minerals, are washed down through the soil. This process is called leaching. Minerals are first washed down, or eluviated. Then they are redeposited farther down in the soil, or illuviated. Where it rains less, this process is less marked, so the soil has a different character.

In deserts, where the climate is very dry and hot, water steams off the surface and water in the soil is drawn upward. As it rises, it carries salts in the soil up with it. This makes the soil's upper layers very salty.

CLOSE-UP *Soil horizons*

As soil matures, distinct layers, or horizons, develop. There are typically five horizons. Scientists label each with a letter, starting with O at the top, going down through A and B (see main photograph), and then C and D deep down. The O horizon is the humus (dead leaves and other organic matter) on the surface. The A horizon is the top layer of proper soil, or topsoil, which is rich in humus. The B horizon is the subsoil and poor in humus but rich in minerals washed down from above. The C horizon is unfertile, weathered rock fragments. The D horizon is solid rock.

ON THE TRACK *Soil profiles*

Soils are identified by their profiles. A profile is a slice down through the soil that shows the different layers. Shown here are profiles for some of the most widespread soil types.

1

1. Chernozem, or prairie soil, forms on the grasslands of American prairies and the Russian steppes. The light rains give the soil a black, humus-rich upper layer.

2

2. Alfisols are well-developed soils with marked horizons that form under the woods and forests of the United States and Europe. Once the trees are cut down, the soils are good for growing crops. But if the soil is overused, the nutrients become depleted. Fertilizers must be added.

3. Histosols form in cold, wet places in the far north of Eurasia and North America, and under bogs and swamps. Things rot so slowly in these conditions that histosols are rich in organic matter. But they are acidic and waterlogged.

3

4

4. Aridosols form in hot deserts. There is so little life here that the soil has almost no humus. Aridosols are very dry and salty and may be topped by a white salt crust.

5

5. Podsols are sandy soils that form under conifer forests in northern Eurasia and North America. The slow pace of life in these cool places makes the topsoil poor in humus and ashy gray in color.

Did you know?
American soil scientists recognize 10,000 different kinds of soils in the United States alone.

Soil acidity

Soils vary in their chemistry. Some soils are very acidic. Some soils are alkali. An alkali is the chemical opposite of an acid. Soils can be acidic because the rain that falls on them is acidic. More often, soils are acidic because they are rich in rotting organic matter and contain a lot of life. Both the decay of organic matter and the breathing of living animals produce carbon dioxide gas. When carbon dioxide dissolves in water, it creates an acid. The acidity of a soil is described in pH numbers from 0 to 14. The lower the pH number, the more acid a soil is. A soil with a pH of 4 is very acidic. A soil with a pH of 7 is neutral. A soil with a pH of 9 is alkaline. Most plants only grow if the pH is between 4 and 10. This project shows a simple way to test soil acidity.

TESTING SOIL ACIDITY

You will need:

✔ Soil samples
✔ A red cabbage
✔ Distilled water
✔ A saucepan
✔ A plate for chopped cabbage
✔ A measuring cup
✔ Small glass jars

Did you know?

Most soil microorganisms like a pH between 6.6 and 7.3, just either side of neutral.

1 Ask an adult to chop up half a red cabbage. Put the cabbage in a saucepan. Pour in 2 pints (about a liter) of distilled water. Ask an adult to boil the cabbage for five minutes, then leave to cool.

2 Drain the liquid from the cabbage into your measuring cup. Pour a little of the liquid into a small jar. This will be the standard to judge the color of your samples by.

3 Take small samples of soil from several different places. Make a note where each came from. Now drop each sample into a separate small jar. Label each jar so you can be sure where each sample came from.

Seeing in depth

Now half fill each jar with red cabbage liquid. Shake the jars gently to mix the soil with the liquid, then leave to stand. With most soils, you will probably see the color of the liquid change quickly. A purple color that nearly matches your standard indicates that the soil sample is neutral. A reddish color indicates that the sample is slightly acidic. A blue or even green color indicates that the sample is alkaline.

When rain forests are cleared, the fragile soils exposed are quickly leached by tropical rain.

Soil is full of grains of natural chemicals called minerals. Many are important for healthy plants. Often, though, minerals are dissolved by rainwater and washed away down through the soil. This is called leaching, and robs plants of vital nutrients. Heavy rainfall increases leaching. So does hot weather, because minerals dissolve more in warm water. This means soils in rainy tropical areas are particularly vulnerable to leaching. When tropical rain forests are cleared for farming, the soils exposed are quickly leached and then become infertile.

Plants and soil

Some plants grow in water. A few grow on other plants. But most plants can only live and grow in soil. Soil provides a secure foothold for their roots. It also provides plants with most of the water and nutrients they need to survive.

Plants need some nutrients in large quantities. These are called macronutrients. They include the gases oxygen, carbon, and nitrogen. They also include minerals such as phosphorus, calcium, and potassium. Plants get oxygen and carbon from the air, but all the rest come from soil—including nitrogen (see Close-up: Plants and nitrogen). Soil also gives plants small but vital amounts of other minerals. These include iron, cobalt, zinc, boron, molybdenum, nickel, manganese, and copper. Plants draw up all these minerals, dissolved in soil water, through their roots.

Did you know?
One of the most common natural fertilizers is the droppings of sea birds, called "guano" in Spanish.

CLOSE-UP *Fertilizers*

Not all soils provide all the nutrients many plants need. Some soils simply do not have enough. Others have enough, but in the wrong balance. Under natural conditions, the range of plants varies with the available nutrients. But gardeners and farmers usually want particular plants, such as colorful flowers or food crops, to grow well. So they may have to add fertilizers to the soil to make up for any lack in nutrients. Fertilizers contain nutrients such as nitrogen, phosphorus, and potassium. There are two kinds of fertilizer: synthetic and organic. Synthetic fertilizers are concentrated salts or minerals. Organic fertilizers come from plants and animals, and include manure, compost, and ground bone.

CLOSE-UP *Plants and nitrogen*

Plants need nitrogen to make vital chemicals called proteins. There is nitrogen in the air, but plants cannot get it. Instead, they rely on certain bacteria, algae, and fungi that can absorb, or "fix," it from soil air. A few plants, such as beans, get nitrogen directly from nitrogen-fixing bacteria on their roots. But most plants get their nitrogen indirectly. The nitrogen fixers break down, or rot, dead plants and animals (1). As they do, they release ammonia, which contains nitrogen, into the soil. Other bacteria take up the ammonia and "nitrify" it (2). That means they turn it into chemicals called nitrates that they release into the soil. Nitrates also contain nitrogen. The nitrates dissolve in soil water and can then be taken up by plant roots (3).

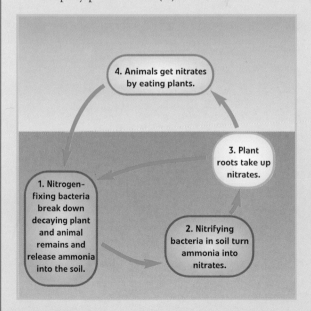

Nitrogen is never lost. It is used by plants (3) and animals (4), then recycled through soil organisms (1 and 2) and through the air (not shown). This is known as the nitrogen cycle. The diagram shows the main elements of the cycle.

Planting vegetables
Crops like this lettuce are less demanding on soil nutrients than others. So the farmer may not need to apply so much fertilizer.

Organic content

Humus is the dark brown, rotten organic matter in the soil. It is made from dead leaves and dead animal bodies and broken down by soil organisms. Without humus, the soil would not be fertile. Humus is food for the micro-organisms that keep the soil's vital chemical processes going. It also helps bind the soil grains into crumbs. Crumbs ensure a soil drains well without drying out. Without crumbs, the soil might quickly turn to dust and blow away. Crumbs also help keep important minerals in the topsoil, where they are needed as food for plants. Farmers and gardeners add manure and compost to soil to keep it rich in organic matter. This project shows a simple way of finding out a soil's organic content.

FINDING SOIL'S ORGANIC CONTENT

You will need:

✔ Several large screw-top jars
✔ Large soil samples from different places
✔ A trowel
✔ A measuring cup for water

1 Scoop soil from each sample into a separate jar. Fill each jar with soil to the same level (about half full). You want to end up with roughly the same amount of soil in each jar.

2 Using the measuring cup, fill one jar about three-fourths full of water. Measure out and add this same amount of water to each of the other jars.

3 Screw the lids securely on the jars. Take the jars outside in case of leakage. Now shake each jar vigorously for about a minute to thoroughly mix the soil and water.

Did you know?
Gardeners often cover the soil in a layer of dry material such as broken bark to keep it from drying out.

Organic floats
Leave the jars to stand. Organic matter floats, but mineral grains do not. So the mineral grains will gradually sink to the bottom of the jar, while organic matter floats to the top. After a day or so, compare the amount of floating material in each jar. This is the soil's organic content. Here, the sample on the right clearly has a much higher organic content.

CLOSE-UP *Tilling the soil*

To grow lettuce like these, farmers till the soil.

Farmers and gardeners often talk about a soil's tilth. Tilth is the physical condition of the soil, and how suitable it is for planting and growing crops. Tilth depends on things such as the soil's crumbliness, how moist and well drained it is, and how well aired it is. To improve tilth, farmers and gardeners turn the soil over, or till it. Gardeners till the soil by turning it over with a fork or spade. Farmers till it by plowing. This works in the short term. In the long term, however, tilling can actually worsen tilth by compacting the soil and breaking up crumbs.

Microscopic soil life

Soil is teeming with life. Just one pound (less than half a kilogram) of soil can be home to 250 billion living things, or organisms. What's more, the range of creatures is diverse. Some scientists think there can be more than 10,000 different types of organisms in one gram of soil (about 0.03 of an ounce).

Many soil organisms, though, are so small they can only be seen with a magnifying glass. These include tiny insectlike creatures such as mites and springtails, and even tinier roundworms, or nematodes. Most organisms are even smaller still and can only be seen with a microscope. They include a huge range of bacteria and fungi.

Although bacteria and fungi are tiny, they play a vital role in the life of the soil. Some, like azobacter, help take, or fix, nitrogen from the air, so plants can use it. Mycorrhizal fungi help make the mineral phosphorus available for plants. Bacteria such as *Bacillus thuringiensis* release a poison that helps keep down the numbers of insects that damage crops.

Not all microorganisms are helpful, though. Rust fungi create rust-colored patches on leaves. Rhizoctonia fungus makes tomato roots rot. Burkholderia bacteria make onion roots rot.

CLOSE-UP *Fungi*

Fungi get their food by breaking down the tissues of living or dead plants and animals. They absorb juices from their host through tangled threads called hyphae. Most fungi are microscopic. Only a few grow large bodies above ground like toadstools and mushrooms, and the fungi shown at right. Many fungi grow on or near plant roots, including many kinds of mycorrhizal fungi. Mycorrhizal means "fungus root." These fungi live in a two-way relationship with their host plant. They take sugar from the plant. In return, they help the plant take up phosphorus and nitrogen. The most common of these fungi are endomycorrhizzae, which live inside roots. Ectomycorrhizae live on roots of plants such as pine trees.

Living on roots

A thin layer of soil clings to the roots of plants. This is called the rhizosphere. The rhizosphere is actually a large area, because plants have so many root fibers. A hundred times more microorganisms live there than in all the rest of the soil.

In fact, most plants have mycorrhizal fungi living on or in their roots (see Close-up: Fungi). Plants such as beans also have rhizobia bacteria that live right inside their roots. The rhizobia form balls, or nodules, on the roots.

Most of these microorganisms have a close relationship with the plant. The plant gives them food, and they give the plant vital nutrients such as nitrogen. This kind of relationship is called a mutualism.

ON THE TRACK *Soil bugs*

In one pound (just less than half a kilogram) of soil, there are typically 250 million creatures much bigger than bacteria, but mostly too small to see with the naked eye. Scientists call these mesofauna. The biggest and easiest to see are mites and springtails—a few are just visible with a good magnifying glass.

1

1. Rotifers are small organisms that cling to soil grains or swim through films of water around the grains. They get the "roti" part of their name from the hairlike fringe around the mouth, which looks like a rotating wheel.

2. Vorticellas are tiny bell-shaped protists (microorganisms) that live in wet soil. They eat bacteria and other tiny organisms, and move along by rippling their long tails.

2

3. Springtails are tiny wingless insects that live in soil. They have six legs and a springy forked tail they can use to jump away from predators. They feed on plant debris, fungi, and other small organisms.

3

4. Mites are the most common of all the mesofauna. They look like insects, but have eight legs and are related to spiders. Many live on plant debris or fungi. Some, though, hunt nematode worms and other small creatures.

Did you know?

There are more different kinds of organisms living in a handful of soil than there are types of mammals around the world.

Making compost

Compost is a mixture of soil and partly decayed organic matter. Gardeners and farmers use it to improve soil. Adding compost to soil gives it extra nitrogen and other plant nutrients. It also helps soil drain better and makes it easier to dig in.

Compost is made by piling together various organic materials and letting them slowly rot. All organic matter rots eventually as it is consumed by bacteria and fungi. Putting it in a pile speeds the process up. In fact, the process is so energetic a compost pile gets warm inside.

Many gardens have compost piles or boxes. They are a good place to dispose of garden waste, grass clippings, and vegetable scraps from the kitchen. This project shows how to make your own compost pile.

MAKING A COMPOST PILE

You will need:

✔ Brown material such as dead leaves, dried plants, pine needles, and newspaper

✔ Green material such as grass clippings, green plants, cabbage leaves

✔ A pit in the yard about 18 inches (45 cm) deep or a well-ventilated bin or box

✔ A plant sprayer

✔ A trowel

1 Dig a pit in your backyard* then pile in a layer of brown material. Brown material is dead, dried plant parts like leaves and pine needles, and also newspaper strips. These are all rich in carbon.

* A glass tank is used here so that you can see what is going on.

2 Make sure everything is torn up into fairly small pieces, especially newspaper. This speeds up the process of decay. Now spray the layer of brown material thoroughly with water.

3 Now add a layer of green material. This is fresh, recently living bits of plants, such as recently cut leaves, grass clippings, and vegetable scraps. Green material is high in nitrogen.

CLOSE-UP *Making soil from garbage*

The world's towns and villages generate so much garbage that it is hard to know what to do with it all. Some can be treated, or recycled, so it can be used again. Some kinds of solid garbage can also be turned into compost that can be added to soil. Garbage composting is not quite the same as the compost pile in a garden. The garbage must be sorted, ground up, and laid in long piles on the ground. But like the garden compost pile, the process relies on natural organisms to break down the waste into compost. A quarter of all waste from towns in the United States is now either recycled or turned into compost.

Building up the pile

Spray the green layer, then build up alternate layers of brown and green, spraying each as you go. Now add a handful of good soil. This contains microorganisms that will help get the process of decay going. Stick a fork into the compost and turn it over every few weeks. This keeps it well aired and speeds the decay. Spray it with water if the weather is dry. After a month or so, the brown and green stuff will have decayed and become crumbly compost.

Worms and snails

Soil is a rich habitat for a host of small creatures called invertebrates. They include worms, slugs, snails, centipedes, millipedes, woodlice, and many different insects. Invertebrates are creatures that do not have a backbone. In fact, most invertebrates do not have any bones at all. Some have a tough shell, or hard casing, to support or protect them. Many, like worms and slugs, are entirely soft. Earthworms rely on the soil to protect them.

Earthworms

Earthworms play a vital role in the soil. As they tunnel through the soil, they open it up for air and water, and mix everything up thoroughly. Worms also break down organic matter into a form that plants can use to grow.

Worms eat their way through the soil, swallowing any material in their path. They digest any dead remains the soil contains, and push out a rich and fertile mix called a cast at their rear. It might seem surprising that a creature as small as a worm can have much effect. But there are so many worms in the soil that their effect is dramatic. There may be half a million or so worms living in just an acre (0.4. hectares) of soil. Those worms can create 50 tons (about 50 metric tons) of castings in a year. They can also open up many miles of drainways.

CLOSE-UP *Snails*

Garden snails like this are just one of more than 80,000 kinds of snails. They are grouped according to where they live: on land, in freshwater, or in saltwater. Landsnails, like garden snails, live in damp, shady places, on soil under logs, or by ponds and rivers. Freshwater snails live in rivers, ponds, and lakes. Saltwater snails live in the sea. They are by far the largest group, with more than 55,000 different kinds.

ON THE TRACK *Worms and snails*

The soil is home to many kinds of worms and many kinds of mollusks. Mollusks are small creatures with soft sausage-shaped bodies, such as snails and slugs.

1. The click beetle is an insect that lives on the ground. In the first stage of its life, however, it lives in the soil and looks like a worm. At that stage, it is called a wireworm, although it is not really a worm.

2

2. Earthworms are long creatures with bodies divided into rings or segments. They have tiny bristles along their bodies that help them move as they wriggle through the soil. Earthworms are most active in wet weather, when they crawl to the surface to mate.

3. Sometimes called eelworms, nematodes are very tiny worms with long round bodies. They are the most numerous creatures on Earth. There may be 250 million in a pound (less than half a kilogram) of soil. They feed mainly on bacteria and fungi.

3

4. The banana slug is the largest American slug. It lives in rainy conifer forests and other damp, shady places. It feeds on fungi and rotting plants.

4

5. Snails have soft bodies and spiral shells. They slide along on a single, suckerlike foot. They feed on leaves. At night, or after rain, a few snails can quickly chew through an entire plant.

5

Did you know?
Earthworms are hermaphrodites (both male and female). All the same, pairs of them mate to have offspring.

Making a wormery

Ordinary compost piles turn organic matter into compost that can be added to soil to improve it. Worms make compost even faster. Every worm eats and digests up to half its own body weight in waste every day. The worms not only break down waste quickly, they also turn it into a high-quality compost. Worms are making compost in the soil naturally all the time. Many households now make wormeries to put kitchen waste to good use. This project shows how you can make a wormery in a glass container such as a large jar or an old fish tank. This way you not only make valuable compost, you can also study the behavior of the worms close-up. The worms best for making compost are compost worms, not garden earthworms.

MAKING A WORMERY

You will need:

- ✔ An old fish tank or large glass jar
- ✔ A cloth for covering the tank
- ✔ Half a dozen or so compost worms from a garden supplier
- ✔ Fruit and vegetable scraps
- ✔ Damp compost, or damp, scrunched-up newspaper mixed with dirt

1 Lay damp newspaper on the bottom of the tank. Then scoop in some damp, good quality compost. If you only have a little compost, add damp, scrunched-up balls of newspaper.

2 Sprinkle the compost with water, then gently lower the worms onto the compost. If you do not want to touch the worms, ask an adult to do it for you.

3 Now you can feed the worms by scattering scraps on the surface. You can feed them most fruit and vegetable scraps, but not oil, fat, or meat. They do not really like orange or lemon peel, or onion or garlic, either.

4 Add another sprinkling of water. Now cover the tank with a layer of cloth and tape it in place. The cloth should be a light cloth with plenty of air holes. Put the tank away in a cool, dark place and leave for a few weeks.

Wormery in action

Watch your tank over the months. Observe the worms' burrowing habits through the glass. You may soon see their casts (see Worms and snails, page 22) on the surface. You should also see the scraps disappear and the level of compost in the tank build up. You may also notice the number of worms increasing. After about six months, you will have too many worms. Empty half of the mix into the yard. Every few months scoop off the top layer of compost to add to garden soil.

Did you know?

Baby worms are not born. They hatch from cases, or cocoons, much smaller than a grain of rice.

Soil insects and bugs

Soil's rich organic content provides a feast for a host of creatures called arthropods. Arthropods are a big group of mostly small animals. They have a hard body case, or exoskeleton, and several pairs of legs. Insects are a kind of arthropod. So are spiders, millipedes, and centipedes. 12 million arthropods live in the soil under every acre (0.4 hectares) of pastureland. They all play a vital role in the soil, as they turn over the layers and add organic matter.

Beetles

Of all soil-dwelling insects, the most obvious are beetles. Many kinds of ground, or clock, beetles crawl across the soil or burrow right into it. Ground beetles are shiny black beetles that look a little like cockroaches. Some live in burrows and come out at night to hunt for creatures such as caterpillars. A few live all their lives in pockets in the soil. They feed on creatures that live in the topsoil such as root maggots.

Tiger beetles live in burrows, too. But unlike ground beetles, they come out during the day—and, even then, only when it is warm enough.

Many beetles that live above ground lay their eggs in soil, and their grubs live in the soil, too. The grubs are the first, or larval, stage of a beetle's life. They look like short, fat worms. Grubs such as the June beetle

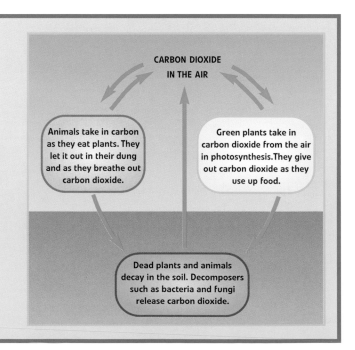

CLOSE-UP *Carbon cycle*

Like other animals, insects play a vital part in the constant recycling of one of life's vital materials: carbon. The carbon cycle begins as green plants and algae take in carbon as carbon dioxide from the air. Plants and algae use carbon to make food using the energy of sunlight in a process called photosynthesis. The plants return some carbon directly to the air as they use their food. Some is returned when plants die and are decomposed by bacteria and fungi. The rest goes back to the air through animals. Animals such as insects and grazing animals eat plants. The animals then release carbon dioxide into the air as they breathe out. Animal dung also contains carbon. As the dung breaks down, carbon returns to the air.

CARBON DIOXIDE IN THE AIR

Animals take in carbon as they eat plants. They let it out in their dung and as they breathe out carbon dioxide.

Green plants take in carbon dioxide from the air in photosynthesis. They give out carbon dioxide as they use up food.

Dead plants and animals decay in the soil. Decomposers such as bacteria and fungi release carbon dioxide.

Despite their fearsome jaws, male stag beetles are harmless vegetarians that feed on tree sap. Like many other beetles, females lay their eggs in soil.

grub and the click beetle grub, or wireworm, are considered pests because they damage crops with their burrowing.

Ants and termites

Beetles live mainly on the soil surface, but ants and termites burrow right into the ground. Ants are usually tiny, wingless insects for most of their lives. Some are hunters. Some feed on plant matter. Many are scavengers and feed on what they can find. Ants live in huge colonies. The nests of those that nest in the ground can extend far through the soil. The nest mounds of ants such as fire ants make them pests where wheat and other cereal crops are grown.

Like ants, termites are usually wingless insects that live in huge colonies. Like ants, too, they are expert tunnelers in soil. But termites only live in warm parts of the world. The nest mounds they build are huge. They are often dug deep into the soil, and built up high above the ground.

Did you know?
Ants can sometimes lift up to 50 times their own weight. That is like a child lifting two small cars!

Burrowing animals

The soil is not only home to tiny creatures. Some relatively large animals burrow into it and make their homes there. These larger animals, called macrofauna, include ground squirrels, prairie dogs, and pocket gophers. Others are badgers, shrews, deer mice, and voles.

The soil gives these animals a place to hide from their enemies. It also shelters them from extreme weather. The animals do their part to help the soil, too. As they dig their tunnels and burrows, they loosen the soil and open up spaces for air and water.

Burrowing rodents

Many burrowers are rodents. Rodents are small, furry animals with two pairs of sharp front teeth for gnawing. The teeth grow all the time to make up for wear. Many burrowing rodents are well equipped for life in soil. They have narrow bodies for slipping easily down tunnels. Their teeth and claws are sharp for scratching away soil. Their feet are spadelike for digging. Many have eyes and ears that can be closed and hidden to keep flying dirt from getting in.

Did you know?

Pocket gophers can close their mouths behind their teeth, and use their teeth for digging without swallowing dirt.

Did you know?
Digging in the soil is such hard work that an active mole must eat about half its own body weight every day.

CLOSE-UP *Prairie dogs*

Black-tailed prairie dogs are ground squirrels that live under the Great Plains in giant colonies known as towns. Each town is a huge network of burrows, and may cover thousands of square yards. Prairie dogs are great diggers, and their burrows have numerous entrances and dens. These rodents pile the earth they dig up into mounds next to the entrances. The mounds not only act as lookout posts but are places of refuge in times of flooding.

Burrowing animals live everywhere, but are especially common in the prairies. There are so few trees there and so little shelter, that many animals burrow into the ground. They include prairie dogs, Richardson and thirteen-lined ground squirrels, and pocket gophers. Pocket gophers are often mistaken for moles because the dirt mounds they leave on the surface look like mole mounds.

Mole eating earthworm
Moles are great diggers, with broad, spadelike forefeet and strong shoulders. They have poor eyesight but a good sense of smell, and feel around with their snouts to find earthworms to eat.

Soil creatures

MAMMALS

The largest soil animals are burrowing mammals such as gophers and moles.

Distinguishing features:
- Warm blood, fur, four legs, two eyes.

Burrowing mammals: Rodents, Insectivores
Burrowing mammals belong to two main groups: rodents such as mice and prairie dogs, and insectivores such as moles and shrews.
Burrowing mammals include: *Gophers, badgers*

ARTHROPODS

The easiest soil animals to see are arthropods such as insects, millipedes, and spiders.

Distinguishing features:
- A hard body case, three or more pairs of legs.

Arthropods: Arthropoda
The 800,000 or so arthropods include insects, mites, spiders, and crustaceans such as crabs. They go through dramatic changes in their life cycle.
Arthropods include: *Beetles, ants, woodlice, mites*

WORMS & MOLLUSKS

Soil contains many creatures with soft, sausage-shaped bodies, such as worms.

Distinguishing feature
- Long, soft bodies.

Worms and Mollusks: Various animal groups
Worms have long, thin, soft bodies. Mollusks are slightly fatter and often have a large pad or "foot" underneath. Many mollusks also have shells.
Worms & mollusks include: *Earthworms, snails, slugs*

FUNGI

Fungi often grow in the soil, feed on living, dead, or rotting matter.

Distinguishing feature:
- Most feed through threads called hyphae.

Fungi: Basidiomycetes, Mycota, Mycorrhizae
Fungi include mushrooms and toadstools, mold and mildew, and microscopic fungi called mycorrhizae, which grow on plant roots.
Fungi include: *Puffballs, glomus intraradix, gigaspora*

ALGAE

Moist soil teems with algae, plantlike organisms too small to see with the naked eye.

Distinguishing feature:
- Algae contain the chemical chlorophyll.

Algae: Various Phyla in Protist Kingdom
Soil algae are microscopic and made of one cell. They use chlorophyll to make food from sunlight, as plants do. They live near the soil surface to be near the sun.
Algaes include: *Green algae, diatoms*

BACTERIA

Microscopic bacteria are the most numerous of all soil creatures by far.

Distinguishing feature:
- The cell has no nucleus (central pocket).

Bacteria: Subkingdom Eubacteria
Eubacteria are the simplest of all living things. They come in three basic shapes: balls, rods, and spirals. Like plants, cyanobacteria (once known as blue-green algae) can make food using sunlight.
Bacteria include: *Rhizobium, Actinomycetes*

Glossary

acid A liquid containing the gas hydrogen that can be sharp tasting or even highly corrosive.

alkali A metal or salt that dissolves in water; the opposite of an acid.

arthropod One of a huge group of mostly small creatures with a hard body case and many legs.

bacterium (plural **bacteria**) Single-celled microscopic organism with no cell nucleus.

carbon cycle The recycling of carbon through the soil and air and soil organisms.

cell Basic unit of life—a microscopic package of liquids surrounded by a membrane or skin.

chlorophyll The green or purple substance in plants that captures the sun's energy.

cyanobacteria Bacteria that can use the sun's energy to make their own food, as plants do.

humus The dark brown part of soil made from the decayed remains of plants and animals.

leaching The slow draining down through the soil of minerals dissolved in water.

microorganism Living thing so small it can only be seen with the aid of a microscope.

mineral Grains of natural chemicals in soil and rocks.

mollusk Small creature such as a snail or slug with a soft body, often protected by a shell.

mycorrhizal fungi Microscopic fungi that grow on or inside plant roots.

nitrogen cycle The recycling of nitrogen through the soil and air and soil organisms.

nitrogen fixers Microorganisms in the soil that soak up nitrogen and make it available for plants to use.

parent material The basic rocks and minerals on which a soil develops.

photosynthesis The way leaves use the sun's energy to make sugar from air and water.

regolith Layer of broken down rock that covers most landscapes under the soil.

rhizosphere The area of soil immediately around the roots of plants.

scree Fallen rock debris at the foot of a hill.

soil horizon One of several distinct horizontal layers in the soil.

soil nutrient Mineral in the soil valuable for plant growth, such as nitrogen and potassium.

soil profile Cross-section down through the soil showing all its horizons.

subsoil Compacted layer of soil beneath the topsoil, usually containing little life.

tillage Plowing or turning over the soil ready for planting with crops or garden plants.

topsoil The upper fertile layer of the soil, rich in living things. This is what plants grow in.

weathering The gradual breaking down of solid rock by the weather.

FURTHER READING:
Raymond Bial. *A Handful of Dirt*. New York: Walker, 2000.
Ed Catherall. *Soil and Rocks*. New York: Wayland, 1990.
Kenneth G. Rainis and Bruce J. Russell. *Guide to Microlife*. New York: Orchard Books, 1998.
Alvin and Virginia Silverstein. *Life in a Bucket of Soil*. Mineola, NY: Dover, 2000.
Corinne Stockley, Kirsten Rogers, Carrie A. Seay. *Illustrated Dictionary of Biology*. Duluth, GA: Usborne, 2001.

Index